Sandwich

IN OLD PHOTOGRAPHS

This streetwise urchin is typical of the child labour common in Victorian times, selling local produce from the farms and smallholdings in the area.

Sandwich

IN OLD PHOTOGRAPHS

Collected by
CHARLES A. WANOSTROCHT

Alan Sutton Publishing Limited
Phoenix Mill · Far Thrupp
Stroud · Gloucestershire

First published 1993

Copyright © Charles A. Wanostrocht 1993

British Library Cataloguing
in Publication Data

Wanostrocht, Charles A.
  Sandwich in Old Photographs
  I. Title
  942.23

  ISBN 0-7509-0213-2

Typeset in 9/10 Sabon
Typesetting and origination by
Alan Sutton Publishing Limited.
Printed in Great Britain by
Redwood Books, Trowbridge

Contents

Introduction   6

1. Town and Cinque Port   9

2. River and Town Defences   23

3. Workmen   37

4. Wartime   45

5. Schools   53

6. Churches   61

7. Hospitals (Almshouses)   71

8. Streets and Houses   77

9. Shops   101

10. Industry   117

11. Recreation   127

12. Miscellaneous   143

    Acknowledgements   160

Introduction

The ancient town and Cinque Port of Sandwich lies on the River Stour some two miles from the sea as the crow flies. The winding nature of the river, however, means a trip of approximately eight miles for any vessel passing up-river to tie up at the Sandwich Quay. The present tranquil air of the town belies the importance of its place in the history of the English nation.

One of the five original Cinque Ports, Sandwich was in medieval times the greatest port in England (apart from London). Its importance diminished only when nature silted up the river, and ships became too large to negotiate safely the many bends and shallows leading to the Sandwich Haven. Into the Haven, and into the town itself with its narrow streets and alleyways, came most of the medieval kings of England together with their Courts and armies, either in defence of these shores, or about to sally forth on continental adventures to enlarge or safeguard England's holdings in France and the Low Countries.

In 1512 Henry VIII demanded to know how many vessels could be accommodated within the Haven. The reply stated that between 500 and 600 hoys could anchor within the Haven while, at every tide, 60 vessels could tie up at the wharves to load and unload men and materials. Although by today's standards these were small vessels, it requires some effort of imagination today, when walking along the quayside with, perhaps, up to thirty pleasure boats anchored alongside, to envisage twenty times this number, all waiting to carry the king and his army on some overseas adventure.

As a Head Port of the Confederation of the Cinque Ports, Sandwich played a leading part when England was growing into a powerful nation from the time of the Norman invasion to the great explosion of power in Tudor times. Situated in the south-east corner of England, the Ports were in an ideal position to defend these shores from continental invasion and to provide a springboard for the many excursions to the Continent by the land-hungry monarchs of the time. In return for providing ships and men at the command of the king (usually taken to be fifty-seven ships, complete with men, for fifteen days in any one year), the Ports obtained many privileges from the Crown which raised them above other communities in the country, to such a degree that, at their peak of influence, only the Crown and the Church were more powerful. Freedom from the many onerous taxes imposed by the king – including that of military service – allowed the Ports to amass great wealth, supplemented in no small manner by the facility of trading in other ports and markets free of all taxes, tolls or other charges.

Many smaller communities through the ages allied themselves to one or other of the Head Ports, but the modern Confederation now consists of fourteen members, being the seven Head Ports (Hastings, Sandwich, Dover, Romney and Hythe – together with the two Ancient Towns of Rye and Winchelsea), and seven Corporate Members (Deal, Ramsgate, Folkestone, Faversham, Margate, Lydd and Tenterden), all of whom originally owed allegiance to a Head Port. Sandwich, with its strong sense of tradition, still maintains official links with three other towns who contracted, in medieval times, to pay ship money to the mother port in return for benefiting from the Cinque Port Charters and their various privileges. In the ancient Elizabethan Guildhall of Sandwich, representatives from Brightlingsea, Fordwich and Sarre swear allegiance every year to the mayor and burgesses of the town. One member from each community is confirmed in office as mayor-deputy, which in the past enabled him to exercise the powers of the mayor of Sandwich as chief magistrate within his community. At the same time, the ship money is paid into the medieval moot horn, being 10s. for Brightlingsea, 3s. 4d. for Fordwich and 1s. 8d. for Sarre. Unfortunately, Sarre has, for many centuries, been unable to afford the ship money, and it has become a pleasant tradition for its mayor-deputy, each year, to offer a new excuse for this nonpayment. The ship money is duly recorded in the Annual Accounts of Sandwich Town Council, and there can be few communities in these modern times whose accounts reflect such a direct link with times past.

Apart from the many kings who have visited the town, many famous men have departed or arrived at the port. Not the least of these was Thomas Becket, who left for the Continent in 1164 following his banishment by Henry II, returning in 1170 a few days before his martyrdom in Canterbury Cathedral.

Following the decline of the port in the early sixteenth century, Sandwich was temporarily revived in the reign of Queen Elizabeth I, who gave a warrant to a number of Flemish refugee weaver families (known locally as the Strangers) to settle and work in the town. Their influence on the life of the town can still be seen in the number of Flemish gables on buildings, the well-preserved Dutch House in King Street (formerly called Lukbote Street), and in the shape of the cupola surmounting the tower of St Peter's church, which was rebuilt by the Strangers after it collapsed one Sunday evening in 1661. The Strangers were also responsible for the inauguration and growth of the market garden industry. The fertile alluvial soil all around Sandwich was ideal for a variety of crops – beans, peas, onions, canary, teasel, carrots, lettuce, etc. – which were sent in later years to Covent Garden for national distribution and consumption.

In the seventeenth century many families emigrated from Sandwich to the colonies in the newly discovered continent of America (there are at least four towns in the USA and Canada bearing the name), each family with a certificate signed by the Constable of Dover Castle and by some 'worthy person' from their town of origin.

The temporary revival due to the influx of the Strangers was not to last, and the town must have presented a sorry sight when, during his visit to Sandwich in 1776, John Wesley, the famous preacher, entered in his diary, 'Poor, dry, dead, Sandwich'! In the nineteenth century, however, refusing to pass into oblivion, Sandwich became a small, thriving, market town serving the many farms and small communities in the surrounding countryside and bringing a degree of prosperity to its inhabitants.

The town's maritime associations, practically dormant since Tudor times, were revived in the First World War when the government, needing a safe haven from which to despatch men and materials to France, constructed the port of Richborough at the mouth of the River Stour. Many thousands of tons of materials and battalions of men left Richborough on the new train ferries to arrive safely in France. Again, during the Second World War, sections of the famous Mulberry Harbour were constructed at Richborough, to be floated down the Channel and sunk off Arromanches to provide a safe harbour for the troops and materials landing in Normandy. Several attempts were made after the war to revive Port Richborough as a centre of commerce but they all failed, and there is little trace now of the hectic activity of both wars.

Places of worship within the town reflect the depth of its history. St Clement's church, with its imposing eleventh-century Norman tower of Caen stone, became the parish church in 1948 when the three parishes within the town were combined. St Peter's, in the very centre of the town, has many ancient features. The south aisle was demolished in 1661 when the tower collapsed on to it and was never rebuilt. The tower, however, was rebuilt by the Strangers who topped it with a distinctive cupola. Mud from the river had to be used to make bricks because supplies of stone ran out when the tower was halfway up. St Mary's, the remaining Protestant church, is built on the site of a nunnery which, according to tradition, was established by King Canute in the eleventh century. It was pillaged by raiders on a number of occasions but was always rebuilt and used regularly until 1948, when the three parishes were combined. It is now, together with St Peter's, in the care of the Redundant Churches Fund.

Nonconformists have always been welcomed in Sandwich and there have been, at various times, Methodists, Primitive Methodists, Baptists, Congregationalists and the Salvation Army worshipping here. Only the old Congregational church (now known as the United Reformed church) survives as a place of worship. Built in 1705 at a cost of a mere £400, it incorporates in its construction the masts of a vessel which brought refugee Huguenots to Sandwich. The old Methodist and Baptist chapels have been demolished, the Primitive Methodist chapel in Moat Sole now serves as an ante-natal clinic, having been a public baths for many years, and the Salvation Army Citadel is now a private house. Catholics have never been numerically strong in Sandwich, but a new church was built after the war in St George's Road to replace a wooden structure which had served their faith since 1929. Last, but by no means least, there is the thirteenth-century Chapel of the Hospital of Saint Bartholomew, an extra-parochial foundation situated just outside the town on the Deal–Dover road.

Sandwich is fortunate that it has retained so much of its glorious past, and is one of only fifty towns in the country that is preserved in its entirety within the town walls. No visitor can pass along its narrow streets, with their wealth of medieval buildings, or walk upon the old town walls encircling the town without being impressed by its unique contribution to the history of this country.

SECTION ONE

Town and Cinque Port

The opening of the 'new' toll bridge in 1891. This replaced the previous one of 1839 which had been built when the original bridge of 1759 became unsafe. Although the weight of modern traffic far exceeds anything which could have been envisaged when the original bridge was built to replace the ferry, the original piers remain.

Sandwich gasworks, originally a private company, was taken over by Sandwich Corporation in the 1890s. It continued to operate the gas-making plant until after the Second World War, when North Sea gas was universally supplied. All traces of these works, including the gasholder, have now disappeared, the site being part of the pleasant recreation area at the end of Sandwich Quay.

Sandwich waterworks was opened on 1 May 1894 at Woodnesborough, some two miles from the town, despite strenuous opposition by the owners of the many pumps in the town (who sold the water to residents). The new system brought pure water to every house in the town. The next annual health report showed a dramatic reduction in waterborne diseases such as diphtheria, typhoid and diarrhoea.

Proclamation from the Guildhall of King George V's accession. Most of the population would have been present to hear the town sergeant sound three blasts upon the ancient moot horn before reading the proclamation.

Another view of the crowds gathered on this occasion.

Distribution of coronation mugs: Mayor Charles Watson is handing a mug to young Reg Somerford. Charles Lee, the Town Sergeant, and the Revd G.W. Keesey, the Congregational Minister, stand behind the youngster.

Unveiling the pictures of King George V and Queen Mary. Left to right: -?-, -?-, Charles Lee (Town Sergeant), Mrs Watson (Lady Mayoress), Alderman Charles Watson (Mayor of Sandwich wearing his robes as Baron of the Cinque Ports), Alderman Jacobs (Mayor in 1901), -?-, Alderman Scott (Mayor in 1912), Revd A.M. Chichester (Rector), Revd G.W. Keesey (Congregational Minister).

The traditional Mayor's Sunday Procession which takes place to St Clement's church on the first Sunday following an election. Town Sergeant Jim Craig precedes the mayor, Gilbert S. Martin, in 1933.

Civil Defence exercises were held following the Second World War, when Russia was viewed as the great threat to world peace. Here, setting an example, prominent members of the town are preparing food in a field kitchen in the Cattle Market. Back row, left to right: Mayor G. Cleverly, Alderman J.J. Thomas, Mr H.B. Fleet. Front row: Mrs Cleverly, Mrs Thomas.

The presentation of an illuminated scroll to Alderman E. Turner by the mayor, Alderman J.J. Thomas, for eighteen years' service to the town as councillor, alderman and mayor.

The Freedom of Sandwich was granted to the local RAF station on 5 July 1955. The Freedom Casket is being presented to the commanding officer by the mayor, Alderman J.J. Thomas, in the grounds of Sir Roger Manwood's School.

Confirmation of Deputies. This ancient Cinque Ports ceremony is held each year in the Guildhall, when representatives from Brightlingsea, Fordwich and Sarre visit Sandwich to swear allegiance to the mayor and burgesses, and to pay their ship money to the mother port. On the bench, left to right: Alderman Turner, H.G. Clements (Mayor-Deputy from Sarre), D. Brice (Mayor-Deputy from Fordwich), Q.R. Clark (Mayor-Deputy from Brightlingsea), Mayor Alderman J.J. Thomas, Alderman H. Burch, Alderman A. Warner, Cllr C.O. Fenson (Chairman of Brightlingsea UDC), Mr Fergusson (Rector of Sandwich). Foreground, left to right: -?-, -?-, Cllr Snelling, Demetrius Foster (Deputy Town Clerk), L.N. Watts (Town Clerk), -?-, -?-, Cllr Baxter.

Baron of the Cinque Ports, Mayor Charles Watson, represented Sandwich at the coronation of King George V in 1912. One of the last remaining privileges of the ports, the Honours at Court still entitle the men of the ports to attend upon the sovereign on the occasion of his or her coronation, a tradition dating at least as far back as the reign of King Stephen. The Cinque Ports barons originally carried a canopy over the sovereign but, since the reign of King Edward VII, their privilege has been limited to attending only at the Abbey.

The Court of Brotherhood and Guestling at Sandwich in 1920. All the members of the Confederation attend this ceremony at the speaker's request. The speaker, whose office pre-dates that of the Speaker of the House of Commons, is elected by rotation from the seven Head Ports – Hastings, Sandwich, Dover, Romney, Hythe, Rye and Winchelsea. They are not elected in order of precedence as listed here but in geographical order from west to

east, with each town supplying the speaker once in seven years. It is the first duty of every speaker to summon the Court, when any matters relating to the business of the ports may be discussed. All mayors, with a limited number of councillors, the town clerk and the officers of the ports attend. The colourful ceremony is further enhanced by the presence of the town sergeants in full uniform, each bearing his town mace as his symbol of authority.

Sir Robert Menzies, Lord Warden of the Cinque Ports, received the Freedom of Sandwich in 1967 and is shown here with (left to right) Cllr Ralph Sage (Mayor of Sandwich), Cllr Harold Carr (Mayor of Dover) and Cllr Alastair Lawton (Mayor of Deal).

This silver bell surmounted one corner of the canopy borne by the Cinque Ports barons at the coronation of King George IV, when George Noakes was the baron from Sandwich.

Members of the Confederation processing from the Guildhall to St Clement's following the sitting of the Court of Brotherhood and Guestling in 1920. They are led by the Speaker, Mayor G.C. Solley of Sandwich.

Earl Beacham, Lord Warden of the Cinque Ports, attending a garden party in Sandwich with many of the local worthies in 1930.

The Association of Jewish Refugees visited Sandwich in 1970 to present to the mayor, Cllr Mrs Maughan, a plaque commemorating the town's hospitality to refugees from Nazi oppression who found sanctuary here just before the Second World War. Front row, left to right: Barrie Roberts (Town Clerk), a representative of the Association, Cllr Mrs Maughan (Mayor), Cllr Mrs Gibson (Deputy Mayor).

Remembrance Day 1966. The town's officials gather round the war memorial in Market Street, where the traditional wreath laying takes place. From left to right: the standard bearers, Gordon Busby (Town Sergeant), Cllr R. Sage (Mayor), Mrs Sage (Mayoress), Alderman J. Jezzard, Cllrs L. Page, R. Chesterfield, Mrs P. Leith, Mrs J. Du Boulay, with council officers A. Carney and G. Rowlands. The Marine trumpeter, who sounded the last post, is in the background, right.

SECTION TWO

River and Town Defences

Although no longer the great port it was in medieval times, Sandwich still prospered in the Victorian era with a flourishing coastal trade. Regular services to and from London and other ports carried salt, timber, coal, cement and many other commodities. This picture, and the five following, show the different types of vessel which were a common sight until the turn of the century.

This two-masted vessel came to grief inland of the toll bridge at Guestling Sluice. It was probably turning to return downstream and misjudged the state of the tide.

Trading vessels and barges were a common sight along the quay a hundred years ago. Local men were employed on a piecework basis to load and unload these ships.

More evidence of marine activity. The 'new' toll bridge to the right of the lower picture dates it to later than 1891.

The 'old' toll bridge was built to replace the original one of 1759 and was itself replaced in 1891. The men in the top picture could perhaps have been preparing to go dapping for eels – a thriving local industry. Even after the Second World War many coffin-like boxes, tethered to the quay, floated in the river to keep the eels fresh before they were sent by train to the London markets.

The 'new' toll bridge, built in 1891. The top picture also shows the Barbican, built to the order of King Henry VIII when Sandown, Deal and Walmer castles were constructed. The bridge swings to permit river-borne traffic to proceed upriver. River traffic has priority over road traffic, provided twenty-four hours' notice is given, and prior to the opening of the bypass it was not unusual for traffic to block the town completely when the bridge was swung. At times the traffic jams extended as far as the junction of the Deal and Dover roads to the south and Richborough power station to the north.

The Barbican, Sandwich.

The Barbican, once known as Daveysgate, is probably the most photographed building in Sandwich. Once the home of the toll bridge keeper, it must now be one of the most unusual council houses in the country. The gates at the end of the bridge have long since been removed, but once were closed each day at dusk.

The Fishergate, built *c.* 1384, is the only remaining original fortification gate. The Ship Inn, now a private house, was known as the Admiral Rodney in the eighteenth century.

The original portcullis slots in the Fishergate can still be seen, although the gates themselves vanished many years ago.

The Fishergate stands astride the lane leading from the quay into the town. Thomas Becket would probably have walked along here when he landed at Sandwich in 1170, only a few days before his murder in Canterbury.

The Millwall, as well as being part of the town's defences, once sported two mills which gave it its name. The building on the left (seen here *c.* 1875) is the prison, built in 1829, and demolished fifty years later, with all the prisoners being sent to Canterbury. The gentleman in the top hat on the right is thought to be the prison governor, Mr Hill.

Although swans no longer frequent the Rope Walk, many ducks, and the occasional heron, still provide entertainment for many passers-by.

The old bandstand on the Rope Walk was a favourite place of entertainment between the wars, the adults enjoying the concerts, while the space underneath made a good hidey-hole for the children.

The Rope Walk. Its original use was for making the cordage for the many vessels which traded from the town, or which assembled here for the king's forays to the Continent. During the Second World War, the adjacent ditch was dredged as an anti-tank measure, thus playing an active role in the town's defence.

The Butts has changed little over the years. The nearby fields were once used for practising with the longbow, which gave the English archers their supremacy on the fields of Crécy and Agincourt.

Looking towards the Canterbury Road, only this gentle slope now remains of the high bank of the original defences.

Traces of the old town wall along the quay still remain in a few private gardens along Strand Street. While this gate may well be a later feature, similar gates would have been built into the wall to give access from the quay.

Workmen

Solley's Dairies were well known throughout the area. Charlie Hart is shown here in around 1928, with the milk cart from which he dispensed farm-fresh milk to anyone who came along with a jug.

Coal men in front of the Drill Hall on the quay, *c.* 1890. They are probably engaged in unloading one of the many barges which brought coal to the town before the Kent coalfields were opened.

Wheelwrights were essential to the economy in the days of the horse and cart. This picture might have been taken in a yard in Millwall Place, as old directories indicate that one George Clark owned a wheelwrights business there in 1890 – a matter of only a few yards from the studio of the photographer, William Boyer.

Two masons resting in St Peter's church, which was largely restored in the late 1880s.

A basket-maker at work, *c.* 1890. His work would have been in great demand among the local farmers for transporting hops, peas and many other crops grown in the rich alluvial soil of the surrounding countryside.

Another master craftsman with a selection of his products, *c.* 1940. Tom Carpenter, who owned extensive osier beds on the outskirts of the town, could make anything required by the locals. During the Second World War he was employed in making the supply containers which were dropped during Operation Market Garden – the attack on Arnhem – for the 1st Paratroop Division.

Work of a more peaceful nature: Mrs Lewis spins yarn in the yard of a house in Bowling Street for use at the Sandwich Weavers, which opened in Strand Street in 1928.

Mounting-blocks were widely used throughout the country, the three steps making mounting easy whatever the size of the horse.

An old tinker, photographed in William Boyer's studio, c. 1880. Note particularly the club foot, which might well have been a ploy for sympathy, as careful inspection of the picture shows that the knee of one leg is much higher than the other – perhaps indicating that any limp from the built-up shoe might have been self-induced.

Builders engaged on the 'new' Sir Roger Manwood's School, which opened in 1895 on the edge of the town, after moving from the original Tudor building of 1564 in Strand Street.

The Three Kings pub undergoing a face-lift. It is now a private house, but the old connection with the trade can still be seen in the carved lintel over the yard entrance, which shows a date of 1614 surrounded by grapes and vine leaves.

Before the invention of asphalt for road surfacing, crushed stone was hammered in by the road-menders, seen here in New Street. Labour was cheap in Victorian days, and there was no shortage of men eager to earn a meagre wage despite the hard physical labour involved.

Wartime

The Horton family had seven sons who served both in the Boer War and First World War in the Royal Navy, the Army and the mercantile marine. On 12 February 1900, Queen Victoria sent Mr and Mrs Horton a letter of appreciation of their family's service, together with a donation of £5, which was handed to them by the mayor, Alderman William Hughes. The seven sons, only five of whom are seen in this picture, were: Alfred E. Horton (Master Mariner), Sgt-Major Robert Horton, RA (who was at the siege of Ladysmith), Sgt-Major George Horton (Royal Irish Rifles), Sgt J. Horton (East Kent Regiment) Lt-Commander Frank Horton, RN (who worked his way through the ranks from the lower deck, and who accompanied Scott on his Antarctic Expedition), Cpl Charles Horton (3rd Dragoons), William Horton (Merchant Navy, who drowned at sea in 1889).

This detachment of Royal Engineers came to Sandwich from Deal for an outing, and was photographed outside the Three Colts pub in New Street around 1900.

An officer of the Cinque Port Volunteers visited William Boyer's studio for this picture. The Volunteers were the forerunners of the Territorial Army.

This First World War photograph is a little unusual as it shows an uncle with his niece and nephew. Donald Cole, an expert bicycle mechanic who worked for many years for the firm of Marbrook & Kirby, is seen with Margaret Cora Cole (nicknamed 'Maffi' as she was born at the time of the relief of Mafeking) and Donald Meaden.

A contingent of a Scottish regiment was stationed at Sandwich Bay in 1918 with an anti-aircraft unit as a deterrent to the expected Zeppelin raids.

A small group of soldiers by their lorry in the Cattle Market on 10 January 1917.

An early armoured car manned by the Royal Naval Air Service near Sandwich toll bridge. The RNAS was pressed into service to transport men and cars of this type to Belgium in the early days of the First World War when the Germans almost broke through the Allied lines.

Royal Engineers posing outside one of the large workshops they constructed at Richborough Port.

Train ferries were constructed on site at the new Richborough Port, which was completed by the Royal Engineers in 1916. The work involved cutting across a complete loop of the River Stour to construct the many wharves required. Before peace was declared, many thousands of tons of supplies and over 20,000 troops had been ferried to France without the loss of a single item or man.

A section of the Royal Engineers on a bridge-building exercise during the First World War.

War memorials to commemorate the dead of the First World War were erected in almost every village, town and city in the country. Sandwich memorial is of a unique design by E. May, a local architect, and was built by H. Barlow, a builder in the town for many years. The centrepiece is a magnificent bronze of St George and the Dragon, flanked on either side by the names of those who fell. The narrow Dutch bricks can be seen in many parts of the town, a reminder of the refugees who came here in the sixteenth and seventeenth centuries.

The official unveiling of the War Memorial on 29 November 1920, by the Right Worshipful the Mayor of Sandwich, Alderman George C. Solley.

SECTION FIVE

Schools

Sandwich Primary School in 1877. It is still in use, but only for infants.

These pre-First World War board-school pupils seem a little overawed by the occasion. Harry Walker is seventh from the left in the back row, and is, unfortunately, the only pupil who has been identified.

Primary school boys, *c.* 1920, clearly show the changes of dress which have taken place. Joe Rogers, fourth from the left in the back row, was a stone mason like his father, and worked for many years at Canterbury Cathedral.

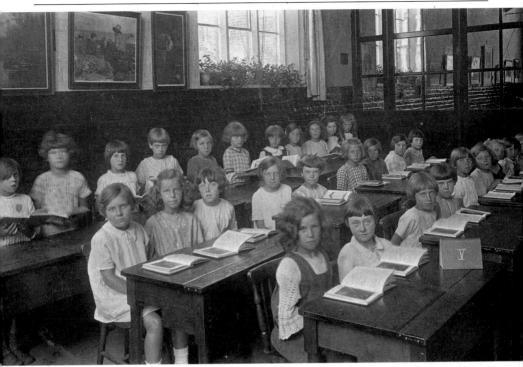

Primary school girls, *c.* 1930. Most have been identified by Mrs Ivy Farra. Back row, left to right: -?- Reynolds, Iris Leith, Peggy Spicer, -?-, Joyce Theoff, Kathy Wright, Ruby French, Helen Wall, Winifred Worth, Beatrice Knott, -?-. Centre row, left to right: Edna Page (m. Miles), Dorothy Hills, Freda Collins, Freda Anderson, Ivy Wanstall (m. Farra), -?-, Iris Smith, Connie Ballard, -?- Card. Front row, left to right: Elsie Ratten, Eileen -?-, Pat Roberts, Joan Gray, Gwen Gisby, Evelyn Whiting, -?-, Phyllis Blake.

Dancing round the maypole, the Primary School, *c.* 1920. Harvey Delves is the little boy on the extreme right, and Ellen Wanstall is fourth from the left. The long-haired girl is Lottie Truscott.

Sir Roger Manwood's School for Boys was built in Strand Street near Canterbury Gate in 1564. It moved to the south of the town in 1895 and this building, known as Manwood Court, is now two private residences.

The new school from the Millwall. Now coeducational, the school caters for upwards of six hundred pupils from Sandwich and the surrounding area.

Forty Manwood's School pupils, with their distinctive Eton-type collars, posed with their masters in 1910.

Sirr's Boys' School was situated in King Street in the centre of the town and was obviously a thriving establishment. Founded around 1874 by Mr Mate, Sirr took over at the turn of the century. The only identified pupil is Arthur Hooper, who is third from the left in the back row.

Miss Fells' School was another of the successful private schools in Sandwich. Miss Fells and Miss Cotten are seen here in Millwall Place with their pupils around 1885. The school disappeared from local directories after 1890, and it is possible that the Stonar House School succeeded it in 1895. Cathie Luckhurst, Clarrie Larkin, Ted and Dick Solley, Ethel Lee, Eddie Simmons and Harvey Street all appear in the picture, but their positions have not been identified.

Principals of Stonar House School in the garden in Upper Strand Street, c. 1920. Mary Callaway was the headmistress and Emily Callaway was the music mistress, and they are shown here with their mother. The school moved across the river to Stonar in 1923.

The 'new' Stonar House School thrived until just before the Second World War, when it moved to Melksham in Wiltshire, where its sound educational traditions are still maintained.

Miss Crook and Miss Blackwell, joint headmistresses of Stonar House School, with Miss Goslin, the matron, photographed around 1925.

SECTION SIX
Churches

St Clement's church has been the parish church since 1948, when the three Sandwich parishes were combined. It has many interesting features, including a late eleventh-century Norman tower of Caen stone.

The Revd Arthur Manners Chichester served both St Clement's and St Mary's churches from 1868 until his death in 1912. His funeral cortège is shown near the Guildhall in the lower picture.

Revd Orlebar Bruce-Payne was rector of St Clement's and St Mary's from 1912 to 1922, and also served as chaplain to St Bartholomew's Hospital for many years.

This old stile on the east side of St Clement's churchyard is now demolished, but the side stones remain.

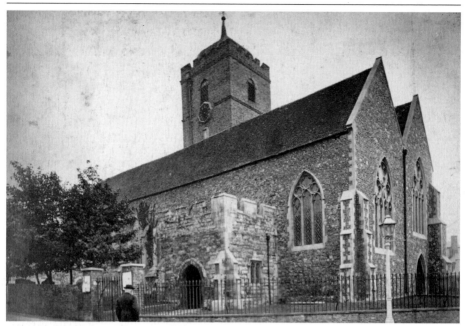

St Peter's church, north side, showing the old octagonal clock which was replaced in 1887 as part of the celebrations for Queen Victoria's Golden Jubilee.

Interior of St Peter's church in 1918. Used by Sir Roger Manwood's School as a chapel for a short period from 1953, the church now stands empty and is cared for by the Redundant Churches Fund.

St Peter's church from Market Street. The narrow bricks of the tower, surmounted by the Dutch-type cupola, clearly show the work of the Strangers, who rebuilt the tower following its collapse in 1661. The curfew is still rung every night at 8 p.m. by a team of volunteers.

The man in the west porch of St Peter's is believed to be a Mr Martin, whose family was closely connected with the church for many years.

St Mary's church is built on the oldest site of Christian worship in Sandwich, which dates back to a monastic church in AD 640.

The Wesleyan chapel in New Street was built before 1871, and catered for part of the strong non-conformist following in the town. It was demolished in the 1960s.

The Sunday school outing from the Wesleyan chapel was an annual event. The probable destination was Sandwich Bay, where the children could play in safety and enjoy a picnic on the extensive sands.

The Congregational church was built in 1705 at a cost of £400 on the site of an old barn belonging to St John's Hospital. It incorporates in its structure the masts of a vessel which brought Huguenot refugees to the town in the seventeenth century.

Another Sunday school outing in 1890, when the pupils of the Congregational Sunday school boarded the string of carts for a happy day out.

In almost every town in England, the Salvation Army had a band which played in every street. G. Maple, third from the left, played in the band for many years.

The Sandwich Salvation Army Band, with the tambourine players, parade in the Cattle Market some time before the First World War.

A typical gathering of children on an outing to nearby Sandwich Bay. The Guilford Hotel, built in 1912, is in the top left-hand corner.

Hospitals (Almshouses)

The entrance to St Bartholomew's Hospital, *c.* 1880. This hospital, founded in 1190, now comprises sixteen houses built around the charming thirteenth-century chapel and provides comfortable housing for some elderly people of Sandwich.

Two views of St Bartholomew's chapel taken before and after the extensive restoration work carried out in 1878–80 under the guidance of Sir Gilbert Scott, the eminent Victorian architect.

A delightful study of a mother with her two children in an old-fashioned baby buggy outside St Bartholomew's chapel. Many Sandwich families still bring their children to this lovely old chapel to be christened.

Brother George Nower and Sister Charlotte Love in front of one of the cottages of St Bartholomew's, *c.* 1950. Every Brother and Sister, when elected to a place in the hospital, swears an oath of allegiance in the chapel, after which the chaplain blesses their house, in a ceremony attended by all the other Brothers and Sisters.

St Bartholomew's bun run, *c.* 1930. This traditional event takes place on St Bartholomew's Day (24 August) every year, when the Sandwich children gather in the hospital grounds and run once round the chapel. On completion of the run, each receives a currant bun which symbolizes the meal that was offered to pilgrims in medieval times when they arrived at the hospital for a night's lodging.

Captain George Raggett and Mrs Bruce-Payne, wife of the chaplain, are seen here on 24 August 1923, distributing buns after the children have completed their run round the chapel.

St Thomas's Hospital, the second of Sandwich's three hospitals (St John's no longer exists), was founded in 1392 by Thomas Ellis, a wealthy draper and generous benefactor to the town. Originally sited near the Cattle Market, the present hospital was built in 1864 in Moat Sole and houses twelve elderly Sandwich residents.

Streets and Houses

The old Guildhall, built in 1579, is situated in the north-east corner of the Cattle Market. The old Guard House can be seen to the left of the picture.

The Guildhall, photographed before the extensive renovations in 1912. The yellow brick fascia was erected around the original Tudor building in the early nineteenth century. An old coaching inn, the Mermaid, appears on the right of the picture.

The Guildhall, c. 1930. In the 1912 restoration the old Guard House was incorporated into the new building, and the whole was given a half-timbered façade. In 1972 a further extension was added, and the L-shaped complex now borders an attractive forecourt where part of the old Cattle Market once stood.

The courtroom of the Guildhall was used continuously for the administration of justice from 1579 to 1987, when the Magistrates' Court moved to Dover. The jury box to the right of the picture folded into the side panelling when not in use – perhaps giving rise to the term 'empanelling the jury'.

The Cattle Market in late Victorian times. Sandwich derived much of its later prosperity from the market activities which continued until the Local Government Act of 1973 came into force and the sale of live animals ceased. Thursday is still market day in the town, but only for stalls selling vegetables, clothing, kitchenware, etc.

These delightful old Flemish-type cottages once bordered the southern edge of the Cattle Market, but were demolished in the period between the Frst and Second World Wars.

The shops bordering the Cattle Market have changed little over the years, apart from the demolition of those buildings which can be seen at the base of St Peter's church tower.

In 1762 a barn behind the New Inn in Delf Street was the site of a theatre. This was replaced in 1817 by a purpose-built theatre which provided entertainment for many years. The New Inn suffered in the Second World War, but was later rebuilt and continues to offer hospitality to locals and visitors alike.

The junction of Cattle Market, Harnet Street and Delf Street. The stepping stones across the corners of this junction were provided for the convenience of pedestrians, particularly the ladies who did not wish to dirty the hems of their long skirts and crinolines, because of the notoriously bad condition of the roadway. Most fashionable ladies carried a long hooked handle with which to lift the hem of their skirts when crossing.

The Black Horse pub in Strand Street was a typical old English pub with low ceilings blackened by years of tobacco smoke and frequented by a loyal clientele of working men. The landlord, Mr Kingsland, is standing at the door with his wife. The building is now a private house.

Some of the regulars of the Black Horse, c. 1950. Standing, left to right: Harry Pay, Alf Fasham, Bert Rogers (a toll-keeper at the toll bridge), Charles Craycraft, Maurice ('Moss') Rogers. Mrs Kingsland, the landlady, is seated. The other member of the group has not been identified.

Market Street, seen here in late Victorian times, has altered little over the years and is still part of the town's main shopping area.

The west end of Market Street with the offices of Emmerson, Brown & Brown, solicitors, in the background and what is now the National Westminster Bank on the left. Both buildings have provided the local townspeople with their services for well over 150 years.

The London & County Bank, *c.* 1880. The public pump standing by the lamp-post is now in the Town Museum.

The pump was rendered obsolete when, despite much opposition from some quarters, Sandwich installed a piped water supply in 1894.

The Westminster Bank, *c.* 1950. The photograph was taken by John Somerville, a local professional photographer, before the merging of the National Provincial and Westminster banks. Mr Emmerson, a prominent Sandwich man, with other local businessmen, provided banking facilities for the town in this building from the early nineteenth century.

A view from the Dover Road, taken from the vicinity of St Bartholomew's Hospital. Note the family group with pram in the bottom corner and the top-hatted gentleman, believed to be the Master of the Hospital, on the left.

This little shop at the junction of the Deal and Dover roads was originally the toll house for the old, inland, toll road from Sandwich to Deal. The original road to Deal ran across the sand dunes and is now preserved as an Ancient Highway.

New Gate once stood at this spot, providing access to the town between the defensive walls of Millwall and Rope Walk. This gate, together with those on the Woodnesborough, Sandown and Canterbury roads, was demolished in the late eighteenth century.

Hibbert's garage stood close to the main level crossing on the Deal to Dover road. Mr Hibbert, as well as running his garage business, also contracted to service some of the railway equipment used by the Guildford Tramway just prior to the First World War.

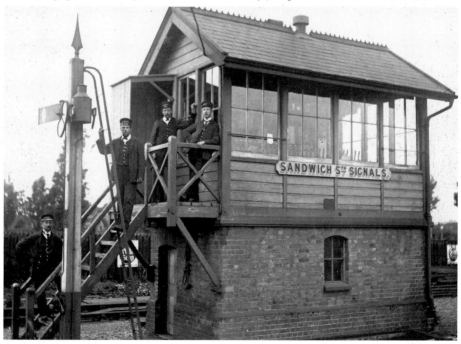

This signal-box of around 1905 was demolished in 1936, leaving a single main box on the Dover Road crossing. John Meacher is one of the members of staff at the far right of the platform.

The Bull's Head pub in Bowling Street appeared in local directories until the First World War, but it is now a private house. This picture was taken around 1870.

New Street, looking towards the town centre. The Wesleyan chapel on the right of the picture was demolished in the 1960s.

Galliard Street, looking towards The Chain in the background. In 1429 the Corporation maintained a brothel here for the use of the many sailors and merchants visiting the town. The girls were safeguarded from exploitation by strict rules laid down, and rigidly enforced, by the mayor and jurats.

The entrance to St Clement's churchyard from Church Street St Clement's. The houses have altered little since this photograph was taken around 1870, and it is along this street that the civic processions pass when attending the church.

St Peter's Street. Despite the time lapse of around a hundred years between these two photographs little has changed. The entrance to Holy Ghost Alley is to the left of the small group in the lower picture. The old town gaol was on the right-hand side until replaced by the prison built on the Millwall in 1829.

Church Street St Mary's is one of the many narrow streets leading from Strand Street to the town centre. The jettied building in the centre is the Old Drum, once a coaching inn.

Church Street St Mary's, with the church in the background, and a small flock of sheep, probably just purchased in the market, being driven away to pasture on the edge of the town.

The end of King Street, looking into Delf Street, just showing the crossroads which lead into Market Street to the right and, to the left, the quaintly named No-Name Street. In the centre background is the Fleurs-de-Lys Hotel, once much used by the local farmers on market days, and for auctions.

King Street, c. 1870. The old Baptist Hall is shown centre left, before Rose's Supply Stores occupied the site. The light-coloured building next to the hall is the Old Dutch House, built at the time of the influx of Huguenot refugees into the town.

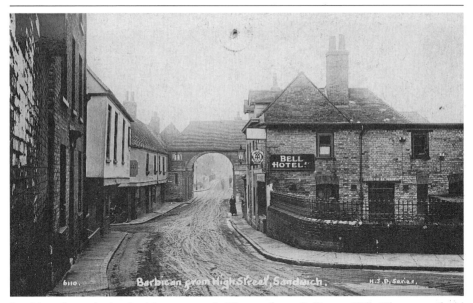

Looking through the Barbican towards Thanet from Pellicane Hill. The row of old buildings on the right-hand side was demolished in the mid-1920s.

Flint House, High Street, in 1907. It is still easily recognizable today and was for many years the rectory of St Clement's church.

The Pilgrims in Strand Street stands on a very ancient site. There are traces of Norman buildings at the rear, and early medieval merchants' houses in front. Even the more 'modern' fronts date back well over four hundred years.

A double-jettied building in Fisher Street, with the rear of Fishergate in the background, c. 1920. Mr Gisby is holding his shrimping net which he would use at Sandwich Bay after taking the Shrimpers' Path from White Bridge to the sea. This path was the subject of a court enquiry after the Second World War when an attempt was made to close it because it crossed one of the golf courses. A local fisherman, Len Champs, successfully led the opposition to the closure, and the path is still open for public use.

The King's Arms pub in Strand Street stands directly opposite St Mary's church. Once named the Queen's Arms, there is a fine depiction of the arms of Queen Elizabeth I over the door. A corbel depicting the god Pan and dated 1592 can be seen on the corner of the building.

Manwood Court, seen here from the garden, has a fine wall-mounted sundial bearing the date of 1564. Queen Elizabeth I dined here during her visit in 1572.

One of the rooms in Manwood Court, which is now divided into two separate residences.

The King's Lodging is a fine Tudor building with later eighteenth-century additions, and is seen here in the 1880s. It is so called because Henry VIII stayed here on two occasions. The railings were removed in the Second World War, to be replaced by the rather undistinguished brick wall which now hides the house from view.

THE OLD HOUSE
SANDWICH.

From the garden of the King's Lodging – sometimes erroneously called the Old House – Henry VIII's coat of arms can be seen just over the door. The Flemish gable on the right hides the conservatory, and has now been rebuilt into the wall on Strand Street as a gateway to the premises.

This fine view of the King's Lodging can only be gained from the opposite bank of the river.

This linenfold panelling was a renowned feature of the King's Lodging but was, regrettably, sold to America after the Second World War.

This beautiful carving over a chimney breast in the King's Lodging is probably of Flemish origin. Such work was greatly prized in Tudor times and reflected the wealth of the owner. Sir Edward Ringley, whose will is dated 1543, disposed of a number of Flemish tapestries among other items, and could well have commissioned this work.

SECTION NINE
Shops

This pre-Christmas display of birds in Fisher Street would certainly not be permitted under today's hygiene regulations. In the days before refrigerators there would have been a rush of buyers late on a Saturday when the prices were drastically reduced to clear the stock over the weekend.

Stokes's Bakery at the corner of Austens Lane and King Street is still a bakery, with the shop door bearing the old name etched into a glass panel. Mr Stokes, seen in the top picture with his son Walter around 1887, was prominent in the civic life of the town and served for many years as councillor and alderman on the Corporation. He was also a serving member of the Cinque Port Volunteers.

A high-class butcher in Strand Street: Mr H.J. Atwood is pictured in his shop doorway, *c.* 1900. The lady to his left is believed to be his book-keeper.

These champion steers were photographed at the rear of Atwood's shop in 1895, where they would have been slaughtered. On the left is Mr Setterfield, shop manager, with a Mr Holness on the right.

Rose's Supply Stores in King Street was established in the mid-1870s at premises previously occupied by a Baptist hall. This picture of around 1930 shows left to right: Fred Green, Sam Cole, -?-, Walter Wanstall, Hilda Potts (m. Green), Bert Keen, Frank Rose (son of W.R. Rose), Jessie Morris, -?-, Joyce Smith (m. Beeby), -?-, Phyllis Jull (m. Harrop), Alan Jull (later to join the Guards and be one of King George V's pallbearers in 1936), -?-, -?-.

This horse and cart was used for many years to make deliveries to a number of small village shops and pubs in the vicinity of Sandwich.

The International Stores were, as their name implies, found in almost every town of any size throughout the country. Their style of shop-front was universal, and it is impossible to identify any particular shop without some local knowledge. This shop in King Street traded from 1895 until some years after the Second World War. Probably taken some twenty to twenty-five years apart, the similar style of grouping in these photographs is most noticeable. Unfortunately, none of the staff have been identified.

Reeves' Tea House at the junction of King Street and St Peter's Street was one of many similar establishments in the town between the wars. In the busy market town there was plenty of business for all. This photograph was taken in 1920.

Snelling's was a bakers and confectioners in the Cattle Market, the premises still being used today as the XVIth Century Tea House. Mr Snelling was another prominent citizen who served for many years as a town councillor, and was also on the Board of Trustees of the Sandwich United Charities.

Durrant's, in Strand Street, reflects the marine connections of the town, even as late as the 1870s. As well as being a grocer and cheesemonger, and an insurance agent, he did a good trade as ship's chandler to the many small vessels which traded from the Quay.

Y.T. Dann's shop is in the same position in Strand Street as Durrant's above, selling a wide variety of goods. It is a little strange that no mention is made of this business in any of the trade directories from 1830 to 1948.

The Thanet firm of Vye & Son first came to Market Street in 1896 and continued for many years, until sold after the Second World War to one of the chain grocers. This picture was taken around 1920 and shows left to right: Mr Arnold, Mr Rickard, Mr Belsey, Miss Fauchew, Mr Bradley, Mr J. Harvey, Mr Reason, Mr Caspell.

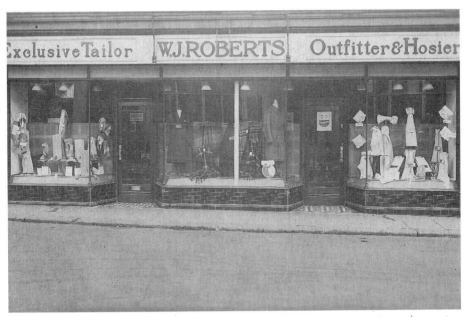

W.J. Roberts' shop opened in the mid-1920s as a quality tailors and outfitters in Market Street, and continued until around 1960 when Mr Roberts died.

One of the last saddlers in Sandwich, Mr Harle was apprenticed to his trade for many years before opening this shop in 1927.

As well as being a first-class saddler, Mr Harle was an enthusiastic collector of horse brasses. His collection, started well before the First World War, was known literally throughout the world, and his displays in the shop window, after he had retired, drew hundreds of admirers. Despite many lucrative offers, Mr Harle resolutely refused to sell any of his collection, but after his death his family loaned a selection of the finest items for display in the Guildhall.

Allgood's Garage, one of the row of buildings demolished in the 1920s, stands to the right of the Barbican. The bottom postcard, depicting an early car (with a Canterbury registration number), was probably given away as an advertising gimmick.

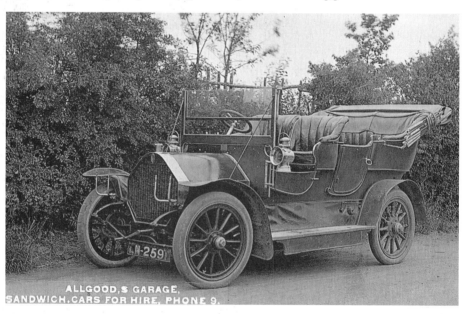

ALLGOOD,S GARAGE,
SANDWICH. CARS FOR HIRE, PHONE 9.

Two more of the many tearooms which thrived in Sandwich from Victorian times to the late 1930s. Brisley's in Strand Street is pictured around 1895, while the Grotto, in King Street, is shown around 1930.

Coleman's shop was in King Street until a few years before the First World War, when J.J. Caspell moved into the premises. Both families had farms in the surrounding area and the shops were a useful outlet for their produce.

Deacon & Son, watchmakers and jewellers, also traded in nearby Deal. Their shop in Market Street is recorded as far back as 1874, but it closed during the First World War.

This view of St Peter's church tower is still easily recognizable today – only the shop names are different.

The Old Dutch House in King Street, when it was occupied by A. Head, tailor. The building is one of many in Sandwich which bears the diamond-shaped plaque indicating one of Kent's historic houses. It is now a private house.

The Hayward family, *c.* 1911 in front of their greengrocers shop at the corner of Potter Street and Strand Street. Mr Henry Hayward is standing to the left of the picture with his wife in front, and one of the boys, Charles, is on the extreme right. Two of the other sons are in military uniform.

Industry

The White Mill is situated just outside the town on the Canterbury road and was working until 1957.

The White Mill is shown here complete with sails in 1960. The last miller was Albert Victor Stanley, whose father, Albert William, was killed early in the Second World War when his clothing caught in the mechanism of the mill and his injuries proved fatal. Bought by the Sandwich Corporation, the mill was saved from demolition and now functions as a Folk Museum, manned by a dedicated band of volunteers.

Situated on the Millwall, this mill was the last survivor of the three which originally worked in this area.

Alfred G. Larkins was the miller when the mill burned down in 1895.

The mill was photographed the day before it burned to the ground. The local press reported, 'It was fortunate that the sails were facing south, otherwise the buildings next to the mill would have been destroyed when the burning sails fell down.'

These houses, with the mill in the background, were built following the demolition of the prison in 1879. They are now hidden from the casual stroller by a belt of quite large trees and bushes.

The *Shamrock*, just prior to launching in 1901, was built by E. Felton & Partners, who traded as shipbuilders and timber merchants for almost a hundred years. It had a somewhat chequered career, being twice renamed as the *Alaric* and then the *Berenice*, before ending its days as a houseboat in a quiet backwater.

After the Second World War, Sandwich made a determined and successful attempt to establish an industrial complex on the Thanet side of the river. Mayor J.J. Thomas was instrumental in urging this project forward and is here seen visiting Nelbarden Ltd, a clothing manufacturer who, among other ranges, contracted much of its output to Marks & Spencer.

The port of Richborough operated briefly after the war, importing materials for constructing an extended runway at Manston Aerodrome, and oil for the new power station. For a short period cattle, brought to Sandwich by rail, were exported from here to the Continent. Mayor Thomas opened the port in the mid-1950s, but it could not compete with the better facilities at nearby Ramsgate. Town Sergeant Jim Craig is on the mayor's left, and Cllr S. Adams is in the bottom right-hand corner.

Mayor Thomas handing over the port flag. The mayoress is sitting on his right.

An aerial view of Pfizer Ltd, taken in 1957. The site has since been developed into one of the largest pharmaceutical production units in the United Kingdom.

One of the successes of the drive to attract industry to Sandwich was the establishment of Pfizer's factory on the site where Pearson, Dorman & Long's factory, followed by the National Coal Board, had stood when the Kent coalfields were in operation. In October 1954 Sir Alexander Fleming, discoverer of penicillin, visited the works and was greeted by Mayor Thomas.

Lord Brabazon was another distinguished visitor to Pfizer's when a new section was opened in 1958.

The local Member of Parliament, Peter Rees QC, visited the Tannery in 1978, and is seen here inspecting a chamois leather hide.

SECTION ELEVEN

Recreation

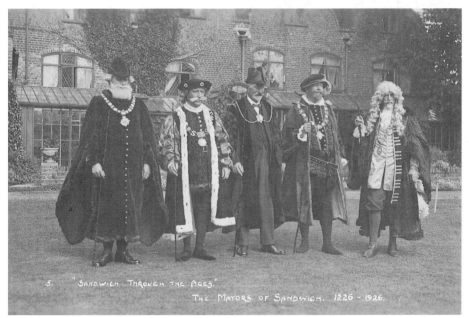

5. "SANDWICH THROUGH THE AGES."
THE MAYORS OF SANDWICH. 1226 - 1926.

The Great Pageant of 1926 was held to celebrate the seven hundredth anniversary of the first recorded mayor in 1226. All the townpeople took part with a will, including the mayor, Alderman Hicks, seen here in the centre with four other 'mayors' representing important dates in the history of the town.

This procession wended its way through the town in 1934 when another pageant – a favourite pastime in Sandwich – was held.

Mrs Andrewes-Uthwatt, later to be Sandwich's first lady mayor in 1929, suitably dressed to take part in the 1926 pageant.

Lady Pearson in period costume in the grounds of the White Friars during the 1934 pageant.

The clown lion tamer in the cage, part of the 1907 Regatta, is Joe Rogers, a stone mason who worked on the new toll bridge in 1891.

The huge crowd on the river bank testifies to the appeal of the frequent regattas, a popular spectacle at the turn of the century.

Possibly the same regatta as in the previous picture; everyone is *en fête*. The *New Trader* offered trips up and down the river during the festivities.

Sandwich Baby Show, 1919. Unfortunately none of the people have been identified.

Many local people enjoyed the sandy beaches of Sandwich Bay before the days of continental holidays. The northward drift of shingle has, however, now almost eliminated the long stretches of sand which were then every youngster's dream.

This obviously well-to-do couple are pictured taking a rest from the gentle pursuit of croquet.

The Victorian age saw the development of a new method of transport – the bicycle. In the early 1870s, before the invention of the pneumatic tyre, the penny-farthing, or 'ordinary', would often have been seen in the streets of the town.

A new form of transport inevitably leads to many different styles until the most convenient is evolved. The young Earl of Guilford poses with his tutor, both on different types of machine.

Enjoying the mobility that cycling offered, many clubs were formed throughout the country, often competing to see how many towns could be visited in one day. This group is seen at the corner of Church Street St Clement's, outside the Cinque Port Arms pub.

Drum and fife bands were a popular form of entertainment. A. Harris's band would have performed many times in the bandstand on the Rope Walk, close to where this picture was taken.

Performing Shakespeare's plays was considered to be very educational for the young. Stonar House School pupils performed *A Midsummer Night's Dream* in the grounds of their school in Upper Strand Street.

Churches of all denominations fostered Mothers' Unions and similar groups. The ladies of St Peter's Mothers' Union are assembled here in the churchyard.

The Congregational church hall was the meeting place for its Women's Federation. The photograph was probably taken around 1910.

The youth movements of Boy Scouts and Girl Guides were very popular during, and in the aftermath of, the First World War. Miss Callaway, one of the principals of Stonar House School, was guide leader in 1916.

The first Girl Guides of Sandwich mustered in 1918 for this photograph, with Miss Callaway easily identifiable in the centre. Their numbers reflect the popularity of the movement in the town.

Built as a memorial to those scouts who fell in the First World War, the St George's Scout Group hut was used until the 1970s. The younger element – the Wolf Cubs – posed for this picture in 1928.

Annual camps were a feature of the Scout movement, intended to teach self-reliance and community spirit. In around 1920 the St George's Group camped at Ebbsfleet in Thanet, some four miles from the town. The scout carts which the scouts would have pulled all the way from Sandwich bearing their tents, gear, and everything necessary for their camp, can be seen in the pictures.

Constructed in 1887 by Dr Laidlaw Purves, the world-famous Royal St George's Golf Links is one of the finest links courses in the world. This view of the clubhouse is dated 1920.

The Lawn Tennis Club has thrived in Sandwich for many years. The large number of men in uniform indicates its popularity in 1915, when this photograph was taken.

Sandwich Football Club had a strong team in 1900, and still attracts many local lads.

Always able to field a strong side, the Cricket Club assembled in 1954 to play the Mayor's Eleven. Many of the Kent team played, as can be seen from the names given below: Standing, left to right: L.D. Nower, A.D. Nower, S.J. Lapish, H. Gardner, A.R. Ansell, D. Hobby, P.J. Green, I.J. Thompson, J. Wheatley, B. Taylor, A. Broom, R. Hopper, G. Belson, J. Baxter, M. Santall, A.W. Atkins, J. Gibson, A. Marshall (Kent), D.Williams. Seated, left to right: D.V.P. Wright (Kent), R. Mayes (Kent), F. Ridgeway (Kent), R. Dovey (Kent), Mayor J.J. Thomas, P. Hearn (Kent), R.S. Hamlin, S. Thomas, E.G. Witherden (Kent).

Sandwich Primary School Football team, 1929–30. Standing, left to right: Mr Williams (Sports Master), Jim Pittock, Percy Clapson, Jack Phillips, Chris Collins, Fred Stockley, 'Archie' Hayson (Headmaster). Seated, left to right: Alfie Brett, Doug Hibbert, Fred Rattan, Ted Blake, Wilf West. Len Daniels is holding the ball.

SECTION TWELVE

Miscellaneous

This novel advertising stunt was spotted in 1921 by Miss Mabel Stokes, then aged 11, who recorded it for ever with her Brownie camera. The cart is at the junction of Galliard Street and New Street.

The great election scandal of 1880. A local enquiry was held into alleged bribery and corruption in the parliamentary election of 1880. The judge lodged at Flint House in High Street and this coach, accompanied by attendants, carried him to the hearing each day.

Sandwich has always been subject to flooding because of its low-lying situation. Both these pictures, taken near the town, show its effects.

The mounting-block seen here still stands outside a house less than a mile from the town. The well turned-out young lady is Miss Henderson, one of the local gentry of the time.

The ten servants shown here exemplify the well-to-do side of society in late Victorian times. Such a staff was by no means unusual, and would have made life very pleasant for a respected tradesman or professional gentleman of the town.

This early car accident in 1913 was a local *cause célèbre*. Bangham's taxi had been engaged in Margate to return one of the Guilford Hotel's waiters to the hotel late one night. The driver misjudged the sharp bend on the road down to Sandwich Bay and finished up in the North Stream.

Another accident occurred on the toll bridge, when Hudson's steam lorry ran a wheel through the cast-iron railings.

Sandwich railway station opened in 1847. The local fly is probably waiting for custom from the London train, which arrived promptly at the station every hour.

Loading a delivery cart at Sandwich railway station with the first coal from Sandown Colliery in 1913.

Wedding groups are always popular, and show the varying style of dress for their period. Nellie Wanstall and Bert Marsh had their wedding party, in 1931, photographed at their house in Richborough Road.

In 1920 young Mr Brooker married Miss Philpott. The family party included Mr and Mrs Small, Mr and Mrs Tulk, Mrs H. Philpott, Mr and Mrs G. Philpott, Mr and Mrs Brooker Snr, Mrs Tuckwell, Mrs Fagg, Mrs Henderson and Mrs Wareham.

Farming and market gardening have flourished around Sandwich for centuries. This steam engine is an early example of mechanization in an industry which before had relied solely upon manpower.

A sad story of mechanization and murder. In 1878 a local farmer, Capt. William Gillow, bought this steam engine to speed up the threshing and similar jobs on his farm at Woodnesborough and, as a result, was able to lay off several of his labourers. One of them, Stephen Gambrill, after visiting a number of public houses in Sandwich one night, decided to break up the machine which had deprived him of his livelihood. Capt. Gillow's son, Richard, had been left on guard and, probably because he had been recognized, Gambrill murdered him. There was no possible defence, and Gambrill was hanged in Maidstone Gaol shortly afterwards. An elaborate tomb, paid for by public subscription, was erected in Woodnesborough churchyard in memory of the murdered man.

Stephen Gambrill was photographed in the studio of William Boyer shortly before the event described above.

St Bartholomew's farm cottages were attached to Home Farm, originally part of the extensive lands owned by St Bartholomew's Hospital. Very prone to flooding, they were demolished in the 1950s.

The Guilford Hotel, named after the Earl of Guilford, was built as a luxury hotel in 1912. A special railway was built across country to carry the materials for its construction. There was some local agitation during the First World War urging its demolition because such a prominent landmark was an obvious target for enemy action. It survived, however, and was a haven for many thousands of golfers enjoying the excellent links in the area, until it was demolished in the 1970s.

Superintendent Stone and his officers in the Sandwich Police Force in 1915. Note the rifles and bandoliers worn by the men in the rear rank – a reminder that the country was at war.

The yard of Atwood's butchers shop in Strand Street, *c.* 1895, where the animals were slaughtered. Mr Atwood stands on the right, with his manager, Mr Setterfield, on the left. Fred Farrier is on the pony, with Joe Page and Jack Bowles standing in the rear.

Members of Sandwich Fire Brigade, *c.* 1870. This horse-drawn appliance is being used to show off the cups won by the crew in an exhibition of skills.

Estate and farm workers are grouped round the above engine which attended its last fire at Waldershare Park, home of the Earl of Guilford, on 30 November 1913.

The first motor fire engine outside the fire station in Harnet Street, with the crew and members of Sandwich Corporation. From left to right: Alderman Hicks, Cllr Martin, -?-, Cllr Watts, fire engine, Alderman Jacobs, Cllr Stokes.

A later machine, with its crew mounted, all wearing their beautifully polished brass helmets. Because of the dangers of electricity, modern helmets are made from a tough, nonconducting, plastic material.

A skilful representation of a medieval house, constructed in the late 1920s in Loop Street by a local builder using old materials. It is difficult now to distinguish it from a genuine Elizabethan house.

Sir Oswald Mosley's Blackshirts, or the British Union of Fascists, had their local office in Strand Street. They attempted to establish a Fascist presence in this country before the Second World War, but without success. This photograph was taken in 1937.

Market gardening flourished in Sandwich from the days of the Elizabethan 'Strangers'. The pea-pickers shown here were employees of Mr Lawrence, a local farmer.

In the days of Sandwich Corporation, all street repairs were undertaken by the local council, and this old steamroller was used throughout the town.

Many Sandwich people still remember this old three-wheeled dustcart, seen here with William Rees Daniels at the wheel.

In the garden of Manwood Court, the Raggett family pose for the camera, *c.* 1912. Note the old-fashioned Bath chair, and the child's rocking horse in the background.

Acknowledgements

Many people have kindly donated photographed to both Sandwich Town Council and Sandwich Local History Society, and it is not possible to name them individually. I would, however, like to record my gratitude to them all for helping to make this book possible. Also, my thanks to everyone who has helped with information and background on many of the older photographs.

I am grateful to the following for permission to reproduce the photographs:

Sandwich Town Council: 10a, 12a and b, 13, 14, 15a and b, 16, 17, 18, 19, 20a and b, 21b, 22a and b, 28b, 30, 32b, 41a, 45, 46a, 49b, 51, 52a, 53, 54b, 57a and b, 58b, 59b, 63a, 65b, 69a, 73b, 78b, 79a, 82a and b, 85b, 91b, 92a, 94a, 98a and b, 99, 100, 102a and b, 106b, 108b, 113a, 115a, 117, 122, 123a and b, 126, 128c, 129, 132b, 140b, 141b, 145a and b, 149b, 152b, 154a, 158a.

Sandwich Local History Society: Front cover, 9, 11a and b, 21a, 23, 25a and b, 26a, 27a and b, 28a, 29, 31b, 32a, 33b, 34, 36, 43a, 52b, 54a, 58a, 59a, 60a and b, 61, 62a, 63b, 64a and b, 65a, 66, 67b, 68a, 71, 72b, 75, 76, 78a, 79b, 80a and b, 81a and b, 83a and b, 84a and b, 85a, 86a and b, 88a and b, 89a and b, 90b, 91a, 93a, 94b, 95, 96a and b, 97a and b, 105, 106a, 109a and b, 113b, 119a and b, 120a and b, 121, 127, 128a and b, 131, 132a, 135a and b, 136a, 137a and b, 140a, 141a, 144, 147a, 148a and b, 150, 151a and b, 152a, 153a, 155a and b, 159.

E.J. Sidery: 2, 24, 35, 38, 39a and b, 40, 42a and b, 44, 46b, 68b, 72a, 73a, 92b, 101,108a, 115b, 130, 133a and b, 134a and b, 146a and b, 157.

R. Dean: 48b, 67a, 69b, 77, 93b, 107a and b, 112a and b, 116a, 136b, 138, 139b, 147b, 154b, 156a

R. Hill: 26b, 31a, 33a, 48a, 50a and b, 70, 90a, 139a.

Miss M. Atwood: 10b, 103a and b, 153b. C. Collins: 142. Mrs J. Court: 49a, 87a. Mrs I. Farra: 55, 56, 62b, 74, 149a. A. Gifford: 41b. Mrs Gosby: 156b. Harle Family: 110, 111. R. Harlow: 118. F. Hayward: 43b, 116b. Mrs V. Johnson: 87b. Mrs M. Laslett: 47, 104. Mrs G. May: 158b. Pfizer Ltd: 124, 125a and b. Mrs Stannard: 114a and b. Miss Stokes: 37, 143.